OXFORD ODDFELLOWS & FUNNY TALES

First published in Great Britain in 1977
by Mudannayake & Breen
Illustrated by Mark Breen

PENNY
PUBLISHING

www.pennypublishing.com

Fourth Edition published in 2000 Edited by Richard Breen
Third Edition published in 1999 Edited by Richard Breen
Compilation copyright © 1996 Penny Publishing Limited
Text copyright © 1977 Breen, Mudannayake
Illustration copyright © 1996 Holte
Designer Tom Gordon

3

FOREWORD

THIS BOOK attempts in a light-hearted fashion to describe the historical developments of the older, world-famous Oxford colleges, their extremely peculiar traditions, and the eccentric people who inhabited them. The stories told about many of these characters are age-old and well-known: in our research we often came across the same story told about many different people, and had to make up our minds which version seemed most likely.

References to all characters, living or dead, are in no way intended to be malicious.

We hope that we have succeeded in faithfully conveying the humorous side of Oxford life, and the true character of the colleges in their historical setting.

"Oxford . . . a red-rose city half as old as time."
Dean Burgon

"Oxford . . . a kind of Fold or Pen
Wherein to herd a Lot of Learned Men."
Hilaire Belloc

CONTENTS

GLOSSARY

BULLDOGS	University police who always accompany the Proctors - never kept as pets.
CAMBRIDGE	A secondary university; somewhere up in the North.
DONS	All Oxford University 'teachers' are known as 'dons'.
FELLOWS	Not 'fellows' as in 'chaps', but high-ranking dons.
HALL	The college refectory.
HEADS OF COLLEGES	Different colleges have different titles for their Heads. To avoid confusion, the title of the Head of the college is written with a capital and other titles with simple letters (ie. The Dean of Christ Church is the Head of Christ Church, while the dean of Trinity is only an official of Trinity.)
OAKS	Rooms in Oxford used to possess both an inner and an outer door, usually made of oak; to 'sport one's oaks' was to keep both firmly shut, and this indicated a wish for privacy.
PORTERS	Every college has one at its gates - Porters are the only people who know everything about everyone.
PROCTORS	Two dons in charge of the University

police or Bulldogs. Their duties include making sure that 'sub-fusc' is worn by students during examinations (dark suit, white bow tie, cap, and gown...).

RAG

To 'rag' is to play practical jokes or to behave obnoxiously towards someone in order to test his powers of endurance.

SCONCE

A sconce was originally a fine imposed for misbehaviour in being boring or anti-social during dinner (ie. talking about women, politics and religion); the bore is required to down without pause a fixed quantity of the drink of his choice (the amount varies between colleges e.g. 3.5 pints in Worcester). If he fails, he has to pay for the drink, but if he succeeds, the man who sconced him is presented with the bill.

SCOUTS

Not members of a youth organisation, but college servants - cherished and respected by dons and students alike.

SEND DOWN

To expel a student from the university, sending him down from the heights of Oxford.

STATUTES

The often strange set of plans, rules and regulations laid down for each college by its founder.

VICE-CHANCELLOR:

The true Head of the University, the 'Chancellor' being only a figurehead.

SAINT JOHN'S COLLEGE

aint John's is undoubtedly the richest college in Oxford; at one time you could go from St. John's Oxford to St. John's Cambridge without leaving St. John's land. When the college's Canterbury Quad was built, its President, Archbishop Laud, showed the wealth of the college by giving a banquet costing one and a half times as much as the building itself.

Laud rode into college every morning on a milk white horse; his students used to point him out, saying, "Behold, St. John's head on a charger." During his time he banned long hair, rope dancers and football from the college. He deplored actors but was fond of putting on plays, especially for royalty. One was so excruciatingly dull that James I

AND DEFINITELY NO ROPE DANCING

fell asleep during it. It was after another, put on for Charles I, that he held his famous banquet. For this great feast the cook cunningly disguised all the baked meats to look like prominent Archbishops, Bishops and Doctors of Divinity. He did not have much trouble with his copy of Laud who was a small, lumpy figure of a man. Once, as Junior Proctor he tried to arrest a drunken tramp for loitering; the man gave him a contemptuous look and growled, "Thou little morsel of justice! Prithee let me alone and be at rest," and the little Archbishop had to scurry away in fright.

At this time Royalist Oxford was being besieged by Cromwell and his Parliamentarians, one of whose cannon balls lodged in the tower over the college gateway, and can still be seen there. When Cromwell won the Civil War, he imposed on St. John's his own Parliamentarian President and Fellows, who were described by the college historian as "lacking nothing . . . save religion, virtue and learning." Laud himself was executed. The skullcap he wore, and the ebony staff he used when mounting the scaffold, were faithfully preserved by the college...

"Every scholar within these walls should cherish brotherly love", said Sir Thomas White who founded St. John's in 1555, having been advised in a dream to build a college at 'a place where three trunks of an elm grew out of one root.' Just such a tree did exist and the college was built round it; it was cut down in the late 17th century by the bursar. Some years later, a student composed a verse about one of his successors who was also fond of chopping down fine old trees:

"Indulgent nature to each kind bestows,
A secret instinct to discern its foes.
A rogue the gallows as his fate forsees,
And bears a like antipathy to trees."

In those days students got up at four in the morning and studied till ten, when dinner was served. 'Dinner' in St. John's meant a penny's worth of beef which was shared among four people. (Rather a far cry

SHALL I CARVE?

from Archbishop Laud's famous dinners). The students then read till five p.m. at which time they had 'supper', which was even more meagre than dinner. A scholar who was served a wafer thin slice of cheese for supper suddenly clapped his hand over his mouth. When asked why, he answered that he was frightened of blowing it away by breathing too hard.

In the late 17th century, St. John's was visited by Admiral Tromp, described as a 'drunken greasy Dutchman'. To make his stay interesting, a drinking match was arranged between him and five worthy St. John's men. To their credit the college men won, and the ancient mariner had to be transported to his room that night in a wheelbarrow.

Francis Treasham, the man who exposed the 'Guy Fawkes plot', was a St. John's student. Instead of being rewarded for his 'patriotism' he was locked up in the Tower of London, and mysteriously poisoned.

The St. John's garden has the largest and most beautifully kept lawn in Oxford. A tourist who was recently admiring it, offered five pounds to the college gardener in return for the secret of success. Pocketing the fiver with a sly grin on his face, the man replied: "Well it's very easy, sir. You just have to roll it, and roll it and roll it... for 400 years."

ROLL-ON!

CHRIST CHURCH

Having suppressed twenty two monasteries to acquire funds, the great Cardinal Wolsey set about building what he planned to be the most magnificent college in Oxford, 'Cardinal's College'. He built the splendid hall (of which there is now an exact copy in Chicago) and the largest kitchen in Oxford, equipped with a gridiron that could roast a whole ox and a chopping block which was then 400 years old... but the Cardinal fell from power, and King Henry VIII acquired the college for himself, refounding it and renaming it 'Christ Church', in 1546.

'NICE NEW KITCHEN', HE SAYS.-
WITH A 400 YEAR OLD
CHOPPING BLOCK!

Ever since then, Christ Church, known as 'the House', has had close connections with the monarch of England, who always stays here when visiting Oxford. During the Civil War, it was at Christ Church that Charles I held his court, and a secret underground passage was cut from the college to Merton, where his Queen was staying.

Henry VIII decreed that the college chapel was also to be the

Cathedral of Oxford, and the Dean and Canons of the Cathedral were to reside in Christ Church (the passage connecting the first and second quads is called 'Killcanon' in their memory, because the winds which whistled through it were cold enough to kill any canon).

The canons were usually an eccentric bunch of men. There was the first Professor of Geology, Dr. Buckland, who, seeing the embalmed heart of Louis XIV in a silver casket, exclaimed "I have eaten many strange things, but never the heart of a king before" and gobbled it up before anyone could stop him; and Canon Jenkyns, who crammed his pockets with toast at dinner every day, so that he could eat it for breakfast the next morning. His house overflowed with books, and his garden with weeds. When asked about the weeds he replied "Oh, I've turned my garden into a bird sanctuary..."

The head of the Cathedral Governing Body, the Dean, was also the head of 'the House'. The most famous Dean was Samuel Fell who completed Tom Quad, the vast front quadrangle (264 feet by 261 feet). Fell was thrown into jail in 1648 by Oliver Cromwell; when they came for his wife she refused to leave the Deanery and had to be carried out like the Queen of Sheba, tied securely to a chair...

John Owen, Dean in 1651, had enough powder in his hair to discharge eight cannons. His successor Dr. John Fell (Samuel's son) expelled William Penn, the Quaker founder of Pennsylvania, and John Locke the philosopher from Christ Church; it was about him that a student Thomas Brown wrote:

"I do not love you, Dr. Fell.
The reason why, I cannot tell.
But this I know and know full well.
I do not love you Dr. Fell."

Dr. Fell instituted the tradition in 1684 of ringing 'Tom' (the great 7 ton bell in the front tower) 101 times at 9.05 p.m. every night, at the end of which the Christ Church gates, and those of every other college, were closed for the night. Any of the 101 Christ Church students still outside used to be heavily fined until an old lady left in her will a sum of money specifically for the payment of those fines. The bell is still rung today at that time.

Another Dean, Cyril Jackson, so liked the sound of the bell that he refused a bishopric to stay on as Dean of Christ Church. A great authoritarian, he allowed no one except the Scouts to wear hats in Tom Quad, for fear that he might by mistake greet them too familiarly. A successor of his, Samuel Smith, once went boating with a close friend, and returned alone; his friend had fallen overboard and clung in desperation to the side of the boat.

"Neither of us could swim," explained Smith, "and if I had not, with great presence of mind, hit him on the head with the boathook, both of us would have been drowned." Thereafter he was known as 'Presence of mind Smith.'

HELP! I CANT SWIM

After Smith came Dean Gaisford, to whom Cyril Jackson said "You will never be a gentleman, but you may succeed with certainty as a scholar." He may have been

13

ungentlemanly, but certainly knew the importance of his position. He was once sent a letter which began, "The Dean of Oriel presents his compliments to the Dean of Christ Church." "Ha!" he snorted, "Alexander the coppersmith presents his compliments to Alexander the Great!"

He even considered himself superior to the Bishop of Oxford whom he once refused entry into the Cathedral. In contrast, a recent Bishop of Oxford had trouble leaving Christ Church after Service some years ago: having driven his little car out through the main gate, he stopped and waited for a gap in the traffic. When he next accelerated, however, the car would not move. He noticed four college toughs standing around the car, but thought nothing of it; in fact they were effortlessly keeping the car suspended one inch above the ground. When they finally let go, the poor Bishop, who had been frantically accelerating till then with no result, shot out into the middle of the road and narrowly avoided collision with a bus.

During Gaisford's time the House had little intellect and even less discipline. The athletic Lord Hillsborough accidentally killed a fellow undergraduate during a 'rag' by breaking his back over a chair; the Marquis of Waterford painted the doors of the Dean and Canons' houses red because they objected to him hunting in pink; the statue of Mercury in the middle of Tom Quad was dressed in the robes of a Doctor of Divinity when the frozen pond surrounding it made it easily accessible. The next day, however, the water thawed and the authorities could not get to it without wading through freezing water, five feet deep.

Some years ago, members of the house drugged and captured a swan, tied a large bowtie round its neck and released it in the pond; and there it was found the next day, foolishly swimming round in circles, not knowing quite what to do next. The statue of Mercury itself was knocked off its pedestal in 1817 by the 14th Earl of Derby in one of his wild escapades. Derby later became Prime Minister of England...

In all, Christ Church has educated 13 Prime Ministers of England, more than twice as many as all the other colleges put together. Lord Roseberry (Prime Minister in 1894) had an allowance of £30,000 a year as a Christ Church undergraduate, and was sent down for refusing to withdraw his own horse from the Derby.

Another Prime Minister, Sir Robert Peel, when an undergraduate, sent a note to a nervous freshman known to be a poor scholar saying that the Vice-Chancellor was appalled by his shoddy work, and was coming the next day to his room to test him on the Greek Testament. The next day Peel arrived at the frightened freshman's rooms, disguised as the Vice-Chancellor (accompanied by his Scout who was disguised as a Bulldog) and having questioned the young man denounced his incompetence and told him that he would probably be sent down. The freshman was so scared that he left Oxford the next day, and was never heard of again.

Lewis Carrol the famous author was Mathematics tutor at Christ Church, the exact location of the rooms in which he lived and wrote his books is kept secret for fear that the present inhabitant of those rooms may be molested by hundreds of curious visitors. Queen Victoria was so impressed after reading 'Alice in Wonderland' that she wrote to Carrol saying that she would be delighted to receive any more of his books. With typical Oxford tact and courtesy he promptly sent her the book he had just finished writing; it was called "The Syllabus of Plane Algebraical Geometry."

PEMBROKE COLLEGE

"Pembroke is the fittest college in town", said a Christ Church Fellow, "for brutes." The college is sometimes even more unflatteringly described as the "coalscuttle of Christ Church", because its buildings are situated immediately across the road from the latter.

It is indeed unfortunate that the Master of Pembroke lives in what used to be Cardinal Wolsey's Almshouses, but this does not seem to have had too depressing an effect, either on him or his dons. It is true that there were two dons who sat side by side at dinner every day but never spoke a word to each other for years and years (when one of them wanted the salt, he would say to the don sitting opposite him, "Excuse me, would you be so kind as to ask the gentleman on my right to pass me the salt?") but the others were all jovial men like that great wit H.L. Drake. When Marett, the Rector of Exeter, an enthusiastic golfer, poked him in the ribs and said:

WOULD YOU ASK THE GENTLEMAN ON MY RIGHT TO STOP PASSING THE SALT ?

"I did something today, Drake, which I bet even *you* haven't done," Drake answered with a perfectly serious face, "Oh, Rector! Surely not ... not *two* holes in one?"

"In this college there are two groups of students", said another Pembroke don, "those who are addicted to reading Greek and drinking water, and those who are addicted to ale, tobacco and puns." The former were the "servitors" or poor scholars, the latter were the "gentlemen commoners" who were wealthy and did little or no work.

After a long and drunken Oxford party one of these gentlemen commoners was wandering round the Pembroke quad late at night, making animal noises, blowing whistles and knocking on all the windows when he was stopped by a Proctor who took his name in order to punish him the next day: after the Proctor had left, however, the din continued with louder and even more unusual noises. Suddenly a second Proctor appeared on the scene, bellowing, "You there! What's your name?" "'Fraid I haven't got one," slurred the student drunkenly. "I gave it to some other idiot ten minutes ago."

Another student who was walking down the street without cap and gown (a wicked crime in those days) was also stopped by a Proctor."And what might your name be?" he was asked. "Julius Caesar," he replied. "Don't be so cheeky, young man!" growled the Proctor. "You must realise," said the student suavely, "that you only asked me what it might be, not what it was."

Dr. Samuel Johnson, "servitor" at Pembroke in 1728, would probably not have found that funny. "The difference," he once said, "between us Servitors and Gentlemen commoners is this, that we are men of wit and no fortune and they are men of fortune and no wit."

YOU SIR, ARE A MAN WITH FORTUNE AND NO WIT!

FUNNY-ENT IT?

He was probably thinking of the poor Pembroke scholar (like himself) who went into an alehouse and asked the barmaid for a loaf of bread; he then asked for a pint of beer, and on receiving it, gave her back the loaf. He calmly drank the beer and was about to leave, when the barmaid asked him for the money.

"What money?" he queried.

"The money for your ale, of course," she answered.

"But I gave you a loaf of bread for it."

"Then pay me for the loaf," she demanded.

"But you have the loaf, so why should I pay for it?" asked the scholar as he strode out of the tavern indignantly, leaving the barmaid scratching her head in bewilderment...

Dr. Johnson lived in a little room on the second floor, over the gateway of Pembroke. Extremely lazy, he never went to lectures and when fined for this he would say, "Sir, you have fined me tuppence for a lecture that was not worth a penny." He preferred instead to stay in his room entertaining friends with his witticisms and drinking endless cups of tea (his vast teapot which would hold up to 20 cups is preserved in the Pembroke collection). When his only pair of shoes wore out he could not afford to buy another, but even so, flew into a violent rage when a well-wisher left a brand-new pair outside his door one morning.

The Methodist minister George Whitefield came to Pembroke just after Johnson, and was even poorer. He fasted twice a week, wore a patched gown and dirty shoes and thought it too extravagant to have his hair powdered. In a fit of religious fervour he once spent two hours praying on his knees in Christ Church meadow on a stormy night. He lived in mortal dread of Satan and hell-fire, and was the object of much amusement in college.

Pembroke students have been more light-hearted in recent years. When the Arctic explorer Nansen was receiving an honorary degree in the Sheldonian Theatre, some Pembroke students lowered on a chain from the upper gallery a large and ferocious-looking Polar bear.

On another occasion some Pembroke medical students were dissecting a human body in a laboratory outside which workmen were busy on a building site. Leaning out of a window one of the students asked the builders, "Would you like us to lend a hand?" "O.K., mate" came the reply. Quick as a flash the student cut a hand off the corpse and flung it through the window.

MAGDALEN COLLEGE

ounded in 1458 by William of Waynflete on the site of a Jewish cemetery, Magdalen College possesses some very unusual features: it has a deer park and is set in extensive gardens through which the river Cherwell runs. In the 18th century, two members of the college, the Lyttleton brothers, were both drowned in the river, one trying to rescue the other. A pillar was erected in their memory in the ante-chapel of the college.

The most outstanding feature of all, however, is its 'singularly venerable tower' (Macaulay), built by Cardinal Wolsey who was junior bursar of the college from 1492 to 1501. From the top of the tower, the Magdalen choir has sung hymns at dawn every May Day since 1501. The college singers were so famous during the Reformation that a choirmaster once brought back in chains to Oxford a country lad with a remarkable voice who was unwilling to join his choir.

The tower has always been a famous Oxford landmark. There is the story of absent-minded Dr. West, the college bursar, who took the coach to London; in those days, one had to change halfway, and so Dr. West got down and entered the village inn. After a few minutes, on seeing a coach about to leave, he rushed out and without realising it, climbed into the same coach going back to Oxford.

I CAN'T HEAR YOU BOY!

Hours later, he woke up from a comfortable snooze to see the singularly venerable tower sailing past his window, and exclaimed, "Well, if I did not know that I was going to London, I could almost swear that *that* was Magdalen tower."

After the tower, in order of magnificence, comes the hall over which such fabulous sums of money were spent that the dons burned all the bills to hide the cost. The food must have been 'acceptable' in the 19th century: Magdalen held the record for the heaviest don (20 stone 10 pounds, probably still unbroken); and Charles Reade, the Vice-President, when in London, used to have his meals sent up from Magdalen in silver dishes. Eccentric behaviour, you might think, but quite common at Magdalen...

Dr. Jonathan Routh was President for sixty three years from 1791 to 1854 and died in his hundredth year.

"Routh scored a hundred but the Fates denied
His wish to score two hundred, so he died"

wrote a budding wit. Up to the age of ninety-four he walked six miles a day and stayed up reading till midnight; he was quite undaunted by the thought of death and once filled a coffin with punch and drank it with a friend in one evening to keep his spirits up! Dr. Routh prided himself on the fact that his aunt knew an old lady who had known King Charles I (in 1648!); an ardent royalist he always fasted on the anniversary of King Charles' execution and was the last man in England to wear a wig. Then there was the student called Stokesley who unsuccessfully

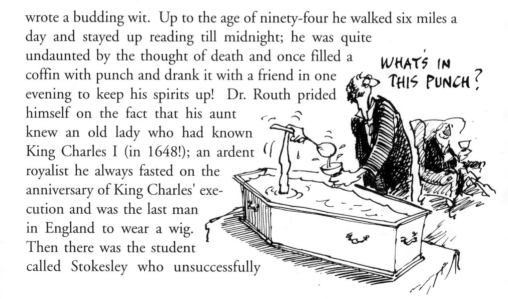

WHAT'S IN THIS PUNCH?

attempted to find hidden treasure by baptising a black cat - he later became Bishop of London. Oscar Wilde was even more eccentric; as an undergraduate at Magdalen, he kept a pet lobster which he took for walks down the High Street on a silver chain.

The college itself kept as pets two extremely ancient tortoises (who were also proud of the fact that they had known Routh who had known etc., etc.). These two, however, came to a sticky if colourful end. During the 1880 General Election, one was painted blue and the other red - the colours of the two main parties (Conservative and Liberal). They died soon after - was it paint poisoning, or an aversion to politics?

A popular game with the students before the First World War was to smuggle a pig into the Junior Common Room, give it a coat of luminous paint and grease its ears, legs and tail. The lights were turned out, and then the fun began... More recently the Magdalen animal-loving tradition was continued by an anatomy tutor - a woman, what's more - who keept a pet python, often wrapped round her neck. When asked why she kept a python she answered, "Oh, because my boa constrictor died."

BETTER DEAD THAN RED

STOP MOANING AND BE GLAD YOURE NOT A PIG !

Touché! But there is more. Dr. Purcell, well-known wit, was once asked to make a pun on the spur of the moment on the word 'King'. "The King is no subject", he snapped. There is the man who invited himself to stay with shy Dr. Beneck, Mendelssohn's grandson, and then refused to leave. One day his dead body was found in the quad, below Beneck's window: when the good doctor was asked for an explanation he shrugged his shoulders and replied, "Oh, I think he jumped out."

Then there is Oscar Wilde, of course, who was greatly disliked by his fellow students - they threw his collection of blue china out of the window and boiled his lobster; not satisfied with that, they tied him up and dragged him all the way up a hill. When they released him and mockingly asked how he felt, he merely answered, "I'm lost in admiration of the view."

Among its other famous people Magdalen has had Prince Henry (son of James 1) Prince Rupert (nephew of King Charles I), Sir Thomas Bodley after whom the Bodleian Library is named, and Cartwright the inventor of the mechanical loom. The poet Addison loved the college so much that he stayed twenty two years while Gibbon, the historian, hated it and left after fourteen months.

One man, however, who will remain at Magdalen forever is Dr. Ellerton. He discovered that one of the gargoyles in the cloistered main quad was the spitting image of himself - a mischievous student had bribed the sculptor to do it. He immediately ordered the face to be scarified beyond recognition. Years later, to his great horror he discovered in his old age that once again he resembled the statue. In fact all the statues in the quad are extremely lifelike; so much so that a tourist once asked 'Moses' for the way out!

STONE ME!

ALL SOULS COLLEGE

If you were invited to a vast and sumptuous banquet, towards the end of which you were confronted by a mouth-watering cherry tart, how would you have disposed of the stones inside those large and succulent cherries? Would you have arranged them daintily and rather boringly round the rim of your plate, or spat them discreetly into your handkerchief, or better still spat them into the fire over the astonished heads of your hosts?

The answer was quite important: this was one of the tests to which you were subjected if you wanted to enter All Souls College. If you passed (like one man, who with great tact and subtlety swallowed all his stones) you were then put through the next test: a gruelling interview in front of four or five dozen of the most brilliant minds in the land...

All Souls College is the most beautiful war memorial in England, built in 1483 in memory of all those who died in henry V's wars for the crown of France. As you might have guessed it is no ordinary college. It has only four undergraduates. The rest of its members, described as having all souls and no bodies, are graduates; and none of your common or garden graduates. To enter All Souls you must be nothing less than a genius with perfect manners. This has made the college the most prestigious academic institution in the country.

However, this was not the case in the bad old days. There was great corruption, because membership was by invitation only. Retiring members frequently sold their places to the highest bidder, whom they persuaded their colleagues to elect. Academic standards slumped. The Fellows were described in 1854 as 'bene nati bene vestiti et moderate docti' (well-born, well-dressed, and moderately educated).

College members rarely, if ever, pursued studies. A porter who was showing some visitors the college's famous Codrington library (the largest room in any Oxford College with a volume of 250,000 cubic feet) was asked if the Fellows actually read all those books. "God bless you no, sir!" replied the Porter, "they don't need to read books. They're gentlemen!" This they undoubtedly were. They walked around in quilted dressing-gowns and kept furry dogs in their rooms. Their favourite Sunday afternoon occupation was to beat up the college under-butler. They made good use of the New Clarendon Press for printing highly obscene Italian engravings by Marc Antonio until the Vice-Chancellor put a stop to it (After all that's what *vice*-Chancellors are for).

In spite of everything, there were a few distinguished Fellows in those days. Sir Christopher Wren, for instance, who designed and installed the famous college sundial at a cost of £32, with its motto: 'Pereunt et imputantur - 'they (the hours) pass and are set to your account' (a quiet word of warning, perhaps, to those quilted dressing-gowns).

In the 20th century, of course, the college has reverted to its original status as a highly distinguished body of academics. One of these, the very refined, very accomplished Dr. Vansittart was once involved in an argument with a boorish specimen from another college, who asked him in a fit of exasperation, "Dr. Vansittart, are you a fool?" To which the doctor replied "Not quite a fool, I think, but very near one."

At the beginning of every century the Fellows of All Souls climb on to the college roof and sing the 'mallard song' to celebrate the fact that a mallard flew out of a drain when the college foundations were being dug. Carrying lighted torches they then search high and low for this mysterious bird, and in the process accidentally smash the 'oaks' of all the unpopular college members in the usual Oxford style, with one rather glaring difference: these are not beardless and callow youths bent on destruction but a group of distinguished old men.

The story is told of one quite atypical member of All Souls who had a party on the 'mallard night' and stingily produced one roasted duck at a dinner for fifteen people. It was a particularly tough old bird, and when he tried to carve it, it hopped off the plate and on to a chair. The host then took a stab at it with his fork but the duck resisted his advances and flew under the table. When one of the guests warned him that his pet cat was also under the table he replied, "That's all right. Don't worry. I've got my foot on it!"

BALLIOL COLLEGE

nce upon a time there was a powerful Baron of the North called John de Balliol who got drunk, as powerful barons often do, and said very naughty things about His Grace the Bishop of Durham. The Bishop, a very holy man, was NOT pleased, and made him apologise, giving him a sound birching on the steps of his cathedral. As a further penance the wicked Baron was told to spend money on a charitable cause. So he provided a home for sixteen poor scholars at Oxford and gave them eight pence a day for pocket money. After his death, his wife the beautiful Lady Devorguilla (of the Scottish royal family) increased the endowment, and that is how Balliol began in 1265.

And now for the story of three Bishops who were punished outside Balliol in the 16th century. They were the Protestants Latimer, Ridley and Cranmer who were burned at the stake for 'heresy' by Queen Mary, in a ditch outside the gates of Balliol at a total cost of thirty seven shillings to the City of Oxford (the blackened and charred gates have been preserved by the college).

A BARBEQUE....FOR US?

27

The memorial erected to the martyrs looks like a church steeple - so much so that a gullible visitor was once persuaded by a student that it was the spire of an underground church, "and this is the entrance", he added, pointing down the steps of the Public Conveniences opposite.

From the 17th century to the end of the 18th century, Balliol went through a stage of slow deterioration. It had never been famous for its architecture - "c'est magnifique mais ce n'est pas la gare" as someone described it - but in the 17th century the buildings were so neglected owing to the apathy and poverty of the college that Dr. Bathurst, President of the neighbouring Trinity college, used to throw stones at the windows 'as if happy to contribute his share in completing the appearance of its ruin'. Even the academic standards left much to be desired. In 1793 when the poet Southey first arrived at Balliol, he was told by his tutor, "you won't learn anything from my lectures, so if you have any studies of your own, you'd better pursue them." Southey later admitted that all he learnt was 'a little swimming and a little boating', and said of the dons 'a waste of wigs and want of wisdom.'

The only students of any intellect in the 18th century were the Scottish scholars sent from Glasgow every year. They were despised for their extreme poverty and 'barbarous dress'. The most famous of these was the economist and philosopher Adam Smith (who used to take tar-water to cure his scurvy and a twitching head). He was disgusted by his treatment and later said that 'most Oxford professors had given up even the pretence of teaching'.

The 19th century was Balliol's golden age, thanks to the efforts of two great eccentrics, Dr. Jenkyns and Dr. Jowett. Dr. Jenkyns, Master of the college from 1819 to 1854, was a great scholar but a very haughty man. Once, when riding down the Banbury Road on his little white pony he was stopped at a 'two-penny' toll-gate. Fumbling in his pockets he realised that he had no money, but the gate-keeper would not let him through.
    "Don't you know who I am?" he thundered, "I am the Master of Balliol!"

"I don't care who you are", replied the gate-keeper shortly, "but you're not the master of tuppence!"

Dr. Jenkyns used to keep tabs on all his students by peeping through their keyholes. One of his victims was Sir William Hamilton who, rushing out of his room one day, discovered Jenkyns crouching outside his door. Furious at this invasion of privacy, he lifted Jenkyns by his coat collars and held him screaming over the balustrade; after terrifying him long enough, Hamilton put him down again exclaiming, "Good God sir! I'm terribly sorry, I had no idea it could be you!"

Another student who showed even less respect was young Blaydes (who later changed his name to Calverley). He was showing the sights of Balliol to some ladies who expressed a desire to see the Master. "That's his window", said Blaydes throwing a stone at it; the window shattered and an angry face appeared. "And that, I believe, is Dr. Jenkyns himself, the Master of Balliol..." Calverley, it seems was very rude. On another occasion, when he could not pay his bills at a tobacconist's, he was told by the shopkeeper to compose, instead, a Latin couplet in praise of his ware. Not knowing Latin, the man proudly displayed Calverley's verse in his shop window: roughly translated it read, "Beware of these cigars, they are evil-smelling cabbages."

In 1870 Balliol elected probably its greatest Master, Dr. Jowett, a small, pink-faced man of uncompromising principles.

'I come first my name is Jowett,
Whatsoever is I know it,
I am Master of this college,
What I know not is not knowledge.'

ran the popular rhyme. A student professing to be an atheist was sent to Jowett for refusing to go to church, and was curtly told by him, "If you do not believe in God by eight tomorrow morning, you'll be sent down." The student saw the light. It is also alleged that Jowett fined a student five shillings for attempting to commit suicide.

In 1873, he offered an exhibition to the seventeen year old, with the initials A.M.R., who wrote the best examination papers. Jowett was horrified when A.M.R. turned out to be a girl, Annie Rogers; accepting her was out of the question, so he presented her with some books instead, and the college invited her to dinner fifty years later! During Jowett's time, it was said that there were three institutions of higher education in England: Oxford, Cambridge and Balliol.

Ronald Knox was a Balliol undergraduate in 1906. A friend of his, Charles Lister, drunk after a twenty first birthday party, was climbing over the wall that separates Balliol from Trinity College, and fell on the dean of Trinity. Not recognising the dean, he swore at him, and was sent down for a term as a result. The next day Ronald Knox organised a mock funeral cortège for his friend, all the way to the station, and inscribed on a stone the epitaph, 'I wist not, brethren, that he was the

SEE YOU AT DINNER ...
IN 1923

A.M.R

High Priest.' (Acts xxiii, 5). The next term, when Lister was dining at Trinity, the dean greeted him with the words, "You won't remember me, I am the High Priest." The Balliol-Trinity rivalry has continued. During the second World War, when there was a shortage of gold paint, Balliol students painted black the gold numerals on the Trinity clock face; and black it had to remain till the end of the war.

Balliol seems to specialise in producing poets and politicians: Matthew Arnold, Swinburne, Hilaire Belloc, Lord Curzon, Sir Edward Grey, Asquith, Harold Macmillan (previous Chancellor of Oxford) and Edward Heath, who was accepted as an organ scholar - the last three were also Prime Ministers of Great Britain!

TRINITY COLLEGE

etween Trinity College and its next door neighbour Balliol, there exists great rivalry which extends at times to bizarre practical jokes played by one on the other. One night some years ago, Balliol suspended from its roof a string of bulbs which flashed on and off in charming technicolour the words "Bloody... Trinity... Bloody... Trinity..." The Trinity wits responded by attaching a large and powerful loudspeaker to the Balliol Chapel, which they switched on at the relevant time, and the service that morning was conducted to the sounds of a well-bred Trinity voice intoning in firm and unmistakably patrician accents the words "Bloody... Balliol... Bloody... Balliol..."

Many years ago, two Christopher Wren ornamental urns in the college's Garden Quad were smashed by a visiting Cambridge rugby team, who, it is alleged, were put up to this act of vandalism by the gentlemen of Balliol.

This rivalry is certainly no new development. When the explorer Sir Richard Burton was at Trinity in the 19th century, he used to be let down on a rope into the Master of Balliol's flower garden, where he would uproot and throw away the choicest specimens and plant marigolds in their place. When at Trinity, Burton refused to shave off his monstrous moustache which was the object of much mirth in college. When warned to keep his oak firmly sported in case he was "ragged", he left his door wide open on purpose, and kept a poker permanently in the fire, to give his adversaries a warm welcome should they decide to visit him; they never did.

Burton was eventually expelled for attending an expressly forbidden race-meet. On receiving the news, he ordered a horse and carriage to his college rooms, loaded his luggage, and drove carefully over the beautiful Trinity flower beds and down the High, blowing kisses at the even more beautiful shop girls.

Walter Savage Landor, Trinity's 18th century poet who caused a sensation in college by refusing to have his hair powdered before dinner like other normal men, was also sent down by the college. The rooms across the quad from his own were inhabited by an obnoxious creature called Leeds, who was a Whig (Liberal socialist of the time). One evening both men were giving wine parties in their rooms and a slanging match began between them. When Leeds cut short the argument by closing the shutters of his window, Landor showed his extreme aversion to Whigs by producing a shotgun and firing at the closed windows. Landor was a crack-shot, but the Whigs were agile, and though nobody was hurt he was expelled...

Dr. Ralph Kettel, prominent 17th century President, had an aversion not only to wigs but also to long hair. He walked around with a wickedly sharp pair of scissors concealed in his muff and used it with devilish cunning on hairy undergraduates. He was just as skilful with the breadknife in the college refectory, which he used when he did not have the scissors handy.

ANYTHING ON IT, ... SIR ?

33

The Doctor was greatly concerned about the welfare of his students; he would secretly leave sums of money on the window-sills of the rooms of impoverished students. He was also fond of peering through their keyholes. In fact this was how he chose his step-daughter's husband, a man called Bathurst, who met with the Doctor's approval because of his extreme thriftiness: he spent all his free hours in his room mending the holes in his stockings. This Bathurst also had one other hobby which the Doctor may not have been aware of: he kept a hen in his room to hatch eggs, and every day opened one 'to discerne the progress and way of Generation'.

During Dr. Kettel's time, Charles I and his court were in Oxford, and the Trinity Gardens were full of lovely lute-playing damsels who frequently attended Chapel half-dressed. Student attendance of the same services, it is said, rose alarmingly . . .

Trinity educated William Pitt (first Earl of Chatham) under whose leadership England colonised America, and Lord North, who was mainly responsible for losing it; also the Lords Baltimore (founders of Newfoundland, Virginia and Maryland) and Earl Alexander of Tunis.

Unforgettable Bishop Stubbs was at Trinity too. Walking down an Oxford street one morning Stubbs saw a sweet angelic little child standing on tiptoe trying vainly to ring the doorbell of a street-front house.

"Oh my child!" exclaimed the Bishop, charmed by this picture of moon-faced innocence, "Let me ring it for you, I can reach", and so saying, rang the bell.

"Now, run like hell!" said the little urchin coarsely, scuttling away and leaving the Bishop to face the brawny sour-faced woman who opened the door, armed with mop and pail. (This is the Oxford version of the well-known story, and hence the only one.)

During his last illness Stubbs was attended by the eminent physician Dr. D'Aeth who had put him on a course of injections. "D'Aeth!" whispered the Bishop in a hoarse dramatic voice one morning when the doctor arrived to give him his injection, "Oh D'Aeth, where is thy sting?"

LINCOLN COLLEGE

hile he was Junior Proctor of the University, Richard Fleming the Bishop of Lincoln greatly admired the teachings of Wycliff. However, he later grew to despise him, dug up and burnt his bones, and most important of all, he founded Lincoln College in 1427 to fight his teachings. Ever since then, the Bishop of Lincoln has been the titular head (called the 'Visitor') of the college.

Lincoln remained poor till Bishop Rotherham, the Visitor of the time, visited it (as most visitors do). When he attended Chapel, the Rector fixed his beady eye on him and in his sermon quoted the Bible: "Behold and visit the vine and complete that which the right hand has planted." Rotherham took the hint and richly endowed the college. As a last humorous gesture he planted a vine in the front quad, which was moved in 1628 to an inner quad where two offshoots, we are told, still survive.

Another Lincoln Rector who was fond of preaching was the Reverend Tatham, one of whose sermons at the University church lasted two and a half hours. A Head of college, the only member of the congregation determined enough to sit it out, was found dead at the end of it.

Tatham was at Lincoln for forty years; at the end of his life he lived at Twyford, outside Oxford, and always rode into town with pigs for sale. (One of his 20th century successors was not interested in animal husbandry, thank God, but he did have porcine proportions: it is alleged that his favourite pair of silk pyjamas (specially made) had a 48 inch waist and 46 inch leg.) The Sub-Rector used to possess a 'scourge of four tails', made of stoutly-plaited whip-cord and capable of drawing blood at every stroke, which he applied frequently to the wayward bottoms of undergraduates.

Undergraduates at Lincoln were sconced by the head of table for swearing at meals, reading papers, quoting three words of Latin or four of Scripture, and punning - Heaven knows what happened when in 1636 a man called Kilbye lost his life in a duel with one Webberley, and students said that 'Kilbye was killed by Webberley' - and one was also sconced for wearing loud and 'trendy' clothes. The main offender in this case was 'Shifter' Goldberg who shuffled around in slippers and wore plum-coloured clothes. He often stayed out all night at drunken parties and came home with the milkman, whom he once threatened to report to the college authorities for not mixing rum with the milk. He did very little work and was so noisy that the man who lived below him reported him to the Rector complaining, "he is always leaving his room - I'm sure that when he goes into his room once, he comes out at least twenty times."

At the other extreme there was Robert Sanderson who read eleven hours a day! He was probably reading the Bible (or War and Peace), remembering the words of Richard Fleming, who founded Lincoln 'to defend the mysteries of the sacred page against these ignorant laics who profane with swinish snouts its most Holy pearls.' Ironically, John Wesley was here for over twenty five years and a Fellow from 1726. He would always get up at four in the morning, even if he had stayed up the night before playing cards, and would study the classics on Monday and Tuesday, Natural Philosophy on Wednesday, Hebrew and Arabic on Thursday, Logic and Metaphysics on Friday, Rhetoric on Saturday, Divinity on Sunday, and of course, Mathematics every day. He is supposed to have preached forty thousand sermons in his life, perhaps one reason for his unpopularity. The story is told that when he met the fashionable and arrogant Beau Nash (of the neighbouring Jesus College) on a narrow pavement, and one of them had to give way, Nash said insolently, "I never make way for a fool."

"Oh, don't you? I always do," replied Wesley, stepping aside. Wesley was unpopular mainly because he attended church services every day; as he came out of Chapel people would throw mud at him (such was the narrow-minded attitude towards religion in the 18th century).

The Lincoln Chapel used to announce its services by a bell which first rang steadily for a few minutes, followed by a few short, sharp strokes (called 'swearing'). Then there was one minute's silence after which the bell rang the number of the day of the month; this gave students enough time to get to Chapel before the service began, except of course on the first of the month!

Sir William Davenant, Shakespeare's godson (or his illegitimate son, as some claim) was a member of Lincoln. His nose was almost non-existent. One day, when he gave alms to a beggar woman, she grasped his hand and obviously thinking that he had lost his nose in some accident or unmentionable illness, gratefully exclaimed, "Oh thank you, sir. May God preserve your sight."

UNIVERSITY COLLEGE

Familiarly known as 'Univ', this college may or may not be the oldest depending on its founder. There are two claims:

'Founded by King Alfred the Great in 872 A.D.' say the members of the college.

'Founded by William of Durham in 1249 A.D.' reply Merton, Balliol and all spoilsports.

The Univ claim is 'reinforced' by the fact that the college owns a portrait, presumed to be Alfred in fancy dress, and maintains that the Venerable Bede studied at the college!

Whatever the truth, 'Alfred' is still a magic word in Univ, as Lord Eldon was to discover in the 18th century. For his nerve-racking final examination in Hebrew and History, after years of study, he was asked just two questions by his examiner (a man dedicated to the advancement of knowledge): "What is the Hebrew for 'the place of the skull'?"

"Could it be... Golgotha?" asked Eldon tentatively.

"Correct, and pray, who is the founder of University college?"

"Alfred", exclaimed Lord Eldon in joyous relief.

"Splendid," said the examiner, "You have passed!"

Not every student, however, was as fortunate in his Finals. Take the case of the scholar who could not answer a single question in the examination. He complained afterwards that he had not been tested on any of the things that he knew, whereupon the examiner tore off an inch of paper, placed it before him and asked him to write on it ALL that he knew.

In 1727, the Court of the King's Bench ruled once and for all that Alfred (not again!) was indeed the founder. The clergy was greatly relieved - otherwise for hundreds of years they might have been thanking the wrong person in their prayers for the foundation of the college.

In the early 19th century Univ quite unwittingly accepted more than its fair share of trouble in the form of Percy Bysshe Shelley, the celebrated poet - then a mere chemist with a wicked sense of humour. Together with his inseparable friend Thomas Hogg, he initiated a short-lived reign of terror. He made his room virtually impregnable by charging the brass door-knob with electricity from his own generator, and took his revenge on objectionable dons by spilling corrosive acid on their priceless carpets. One morning when he was in particularly fine form, Shelley snatched a baby out of its mother's arms in order to test his theories of reincarnation. This startling confrontation between Town and Gown took place on Magdalen bridge, high above the swirling waters of the river Cherwell. Brandishing the baby aloft, he threatened it with extinction to make it divulge the secrets of its previous life.

OOOOPS

ACME GENERATOR

"But he can't speak - he's only a baby," shrieked the mother, with the wisdom for which the Oxford townspeople are renowned.

"Surely he can speak if he wishes to," snapped Shelley, "he's only a few weeks old. He can't have entirely forgotten the use of speech in so short a time."

The end came when Shelley published a pamphlet on 'the necessity of Atheism' and displayed it in a shop window. The college had had enough. He and his friend Hogg were sent down immediately, and this perhaps accounts for the latter's parting words: "Oxford is the seat in which learning sits very comfortably, well thrown back as in an easy chair; and sleeps so soundly that neither you, nor I, nor anyone else can wake her up."

Ironically Univ had not seen the last of Shelley; after his death, the college could not but accept the hideous 'Shelley memorial' presented by Lady Shelley, and to this day it stands - a statue enclosed by a curious glass dome - the last and most impractical joke of all.

In 1872 the college showed that it still had the courage of its convictions by celebrating its Millenary - the thousandth year after its foundation by King Alfred (Oh, enough of Alfred!)

1880 was a memorable year in the history of Univ. The Senior Proctor (nicknamed 'big shaver,' for some obscure reason) woke up one morning to find that the undergraduates had securely fastened his outer door to its frame with impossibly long screws.

Catching sight of the Master of the college in the High Street below he shouted through the window in desperation,

"Master, I'm screwed!"

"Be quiet," came the irate reply, "there's no need to tell everyone."

There was only one way out - through the window. And so it came about that the Proctor had to descend a ladder into the High Street with as much dignity as he could muster amidst the cheers of the populace. This time the whole college was sent down until the culprits owned up.

In the present century Univ students have been rather better known for their wit than for their exploits. Some years ago, two Nigerian professors visiting Oxford asked a Univ don permission to be present when he interviewed the candidates applying for entrance that year. These interviews took place after a particularly stiff written examination. One candidate whose papers had been disastrous, was told that there was no hope for him unless his interview was spectacular. When his turn came, he knocked nervously on the door and was told to come in. Seeing the don sitting at a desk with the Nigerian professors on either side he seized his opportunity; with an enormous grin on his face he strode up to the don and asked,

"Doctor Livingstone I presume?"

It is fair to say that he was given a place on the recommendation of the two visitors.

Clement Attlee, the former Prime Minister, was an undergraduate at Univ and caused the college no trouble; another Prime Minister, Harold Wilson was also here as bursar... the college has continued to prosper and gain in stature - especially 'stature' with the arrival of one of its recent Masters, the monumental Lord Goodman. There have been malicious rumours that a king size bath had to be installed to accommodate the ample proportions of this gentleman, but these are unfounded and smack of 'Alfredism'.

MERTON COLLEGE

From the word go, Merton was small and smart and rich; and always rather condescending, even though other, lesser 'institutions' (Univ.? Balliol?) might have existed before, Merton was unquestionably the first college. Its founder, Walter de Merton, was also involved in building the first Cambridge college, Peterhouse, with strict instructions that its scholars were to follow the example of the Merton ones in every way, but they never did, and perhaps it's just as well.

Merton had stout walls, the first open-shelf library in the world, and students who were gentlemen. In 1487 a scholar called Hugo Shakespeer was ordered to change his name immediately because it was not one that self-respecting gentlemen would have had at the time! Merton changed its mind two centuries later though, when it accepted a William Shakespeare first folio - which is still kept in the library.

In those days there were frequent clashes between the people of the Town, and the students (collectively termed 'the Gown'). The Gown objected to the fish that the Town sold (which stank) and its beer (which was brewed from sewage water). The arguments came to a head on St. Scholastica's day, in 1354, when some scholars in a pub threw beer at the publican's head. The publican was a small man, and the students escaped unscathed, but not for long. The Town turned out in large numbers, fully equipped with bows and arrows, and began to take pot shots at unsuspecting students. The Chancellor of the University appeared in full regalia, in a vain effort to stop the disturbance; they shot him in the behind! At sunset the Town retired for the night to the nether regions of Cowley and Headington.

The next day they returned with another two thousand peasants carrying an ominous black flag, and they proceeded to destroy everything they could lay their hands on. This time the Friars came out to make peace carrying a crucifix and chanting rosaries. No such luck: those fortunate enough to have hair were tonsured, and the bald ones were scalped. The Gown took one look at this and fled into the countryside. All except the Merton students, that is; these hardy gentlemen took refuge within their stout walls - even today one of the quads is called the 'Mob quad' in their memory - and in a last supreme gesture of contempt at the Town beer, they turned their Sacristy into a Brewery.

In the 16th century Elizabeth I visited Merton; on leaving, she said, "Farewell, farewell, dear Oxford! God bless thee and increase thy sons in number, holiness and virtue!" (She obviously felt that prayers were needed). She sent Warden Mann of Merton on a Mission to Spain saying, in one of her rare witty moods, "Philip has sent me a Gooseman" (Guzman, Spanish ambassador in England) "so I will send him a Mann goose."

During the Civil War a Royalist colonel called Windebank was persuaded by his wife and the wives of officers in his regiment to surrender to Parliament the town of Bletchingdon. The poor man was shot for treason by Prince Rupert, against a wall in Merton gardens; there is a path there today called 'Dead Man's Walk'. It was at this time that Queen Henrietta-Maria came to stay at the Warden's lodgings, bringing with her plenty of wine, women and song. The students soon discovered that there were better things in life than books, and Merton became more famous for its scandals than its studies - a reputation carried well into the next century when you could find, at any time of day, extremely charming young ladies strolling leisurely through the college gardens. It was only in 1720 that the authorities realised what was going on and locked the garden gates.

In 1723 a Proctor found a Merton don drinking furtively after midnight in a pub called 'the Mitre' - he was expelled immediately; a few days later the same Proctor discovered a student in the pub, also after midnight; when arrested, the student fell over, dead drunk, exclaiming, "Save the women and children. I'm all right, I can swim."

In recent times Merton kept up the traditions of fine living by employing an ex-Claridges chef who regularly prepared the most exotic dishes to cater for a wide variety of tastes; and there has certainly been a wide variety of dons. H.W. Garrod for instance, who in 1914 was handed a white feather by a young woman in the street who glared at him and said, "How dare you stand there while everyone else is fighting to preserve civilisation?"

"Madam," replied Garrod suavely, "I am the civilisation they are fighting to preserve."

I STILL DON'T LIKE THAT LAMP-POST

There was another Merton don who got up in the middle of the night, crept up High Street and began to dig up a lamp-post which offended his sense of beauty. He was led back to his bed by a kindly policeman who understood the ways of Oxford dons. On another occasion the same man, for a wager, walked down High Street dressed in a Samurai suit. A group of Japanese tourists coming up the street hastily crossed over to the other side.

During the Second World War, there was a Merton student who, when asked the way to Abingdon by an American convoy coming over Magdalene bridge, directed them into Merton Street, a narrow winding path leading to Merton. A few minutes later a second convoy came over the bridge and these trucks he directed into King Edward Street (an even narrower lane) and told them to turn left. There was chaos in Oriel Square where the two met, and it took them a whole day to get out! (See map).

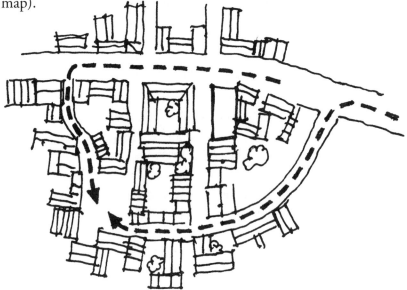

J.R. Tolkien was also a Merton don. Other notabilities include William Harvey who discovered the circulation of the blood, Sir William Berkeley, T.S. Eliot who said "Oxford is all right but I don't like being dead", and Lord Randolph Churchill whose Oxford education was hopelessly inadequate when it came to dealing with such matters as decimal fractions - when he was Chancellor of the Exchequer he had to employ a permanent official whose sole duty was to explain to him the meaning of "those damned dots."

THE QUEEN'S COLLEGE

he most elegant ladies' loos in Oxford can be found at Queen's College - a subtle compliment perhaps to the woman after whom the college is named, Queen Philippa, wife of Edward III. Robert de Egglesfield, her chaplain and confessor, founded Queen's in 1341 for 'honest, chaste, peaceful, humble, considerate poor persons from the North, fit for study and anxious to improve'; or so he hoped. He reckoned without the intense pleasure which North countrymen could derive from beer and rowdy behaviour.

"From the gentlemen in the back quad at Queen's, Good Lord, deliver us," prayed the frightened Univ students when the Queen's mob emerged each morning, hair unwashed and unkempt (even though the statutes provided for a permanent barber in the college) armed with bows, arrows, dogs and musical instruments, all of which were forbidden by the founder. Not every Queen's man, however, felt the same way about these pastimes. One venerable Archbishop of York, Dr Thompson, is reported to have been sent down in 1919 after laying waste the room above his own, and its occupant, who insisted on playing his musical instruments at all hours of the day and night.

The founder also had very definite ideas about his Fellows. There were to be the same number as the apostles, all dressed in crimson robes, and they were to be summoned to hall by the blowing of trumpets, a custom still observed today. This obsession with decorous behaviour nearly had disastrous consequences in 1778 when the West wing of the front quad caught fire in the middle of the night. The quad was soon full of Fellows, scurrying for safety, not in red robes but in nightshirts and long bobbled nightcaps, all except for the Provost, Dr. Fothergill, who was nowhere to be seen. Fearing that he was trapped inside and unable to get out, the Fellows had given up all hope for his safety, when the good Doctor suddenly appeared walking out of the flames, like some emissary from heaven, completely bedecked in wig, gown, cap, armbands and other ecclesiastical trappings, all of which he had carefully put on, while the building was being engulfed by fire.

On the whole, the gods do not seem to have viewed the buildings of Queen's with much favour. On the 11th of June 1970 one of the two stone eagles on the library was completely shattered by lightning.

On another occasion there was a fire in the bursary, where the bursar, it is said, was busy cooking the accounts. Apart from such usual culinary activities, the Queen's College bursar has one age-old duty to perform every New Year's Day; he hands a needle and thread to all members, saying; "Take this and be thrifty." (This is supposed to be a pun in French on the founder's name, 'Egglesfield': 'aiguille'=needle, and 'fil'= thread).

TAKE THIS!... AND BE THRIFTY

Looking back on events, the college's reputation for heartiness and lack of scholarship seems to be totally unjustified. It was a scholar from Queen's, for instance, who, while walking on Shotover Hill reading Aristotle, was attacked by a ferocious wild boar. Instead of running away he rammed the volume down the beast's throat and choked it to death, shouting the words 'Graecum est' (the last words of the book). He then cut off its head and brought this great delicacy back home to dinner. The college celebrates this great event, the triumph of scholarship over brute force, by its Boar's Head dinner which takes place on Christmas night every year.

Then there is Jeremy Bentham, the philosopher, who was so clever that he learnt Latin at the age of three and philosophy at five. He entered Queen's in 1761 when he was thirteen. He was short of money and always badly dressed, and crept around the college in mortal dread of the ghosts lurking on the stairways. Although he hated life at Oxford, it had one good effect on him - it cured him of his love for gambling: "They always forced me to pay when I lost," he said, "and as I could never get the money when I won, I gave up the habit."

Another Queen's man who may not have been clever but was certainly wily, was one evening pursued down High Street by the Proctors for committing an offence. He took refuge on the front steps of Queen's, one of the few places in Oxford where, by tradition, students cannot be arrested. The Proctors, who were convinced that he came from another college and would therefore have to get back to his rooms before midnight, at which point they would apprehend him, waited at the bottom of the steps for one hour, while he hurled abuses at them. On the stroke of midnight, he got up, opened the door of Queen's and disappeared into the college.

Last but not least of all was Walter Pater, whose extreme intelligence was superceded only by his extreme ugliness. His friends formed a 'Committee to Consider what could be Done for the Improvement of Pater's Personal Appearance.' Their first idea, that he should wear a hat at all times, was rejected because he could not wear one in bed. It was finally decided that he should wear a moustache. The end result, they said delightedly, made him look like a 'benevolent dragon.' It was quite true... the capillary growth on Pater's stiff upper lip did much to enhance his looks, and proved once again the age-old proverb that behind every moustache there is an ugly face struggling to get out!

BRASENOSE COLLEGE

This college derives its peculiar name from a brass doorknocker in the shape of a nose with a ring through its nostrils. Nobody knows when this curious knocker first appeared in the college, but in 1334 it was stolen by rebel students who took it with them to Stamford in Lincolnshire. It took the college five centuries to follow its nose to Stamford, where in 1890 it regained the famous knocker by buying up the girls' school to which it then belonged. In the meantime the college had had another made, so today happily it has two knockers.

Dean Hole, aptly described the life the college has traditionally led by writing:

"How jollily, how joyously, we live at B.N.C.!
Our reading is all moonshine, the wind is not more free."

He goes on to say that "the reading men were not such cheery companions as the men who rode, and drove, and played cricket, and wore gay clothing, and smoked fragrant regalias." B.N.C. has persistently tried to achieve high academic and moral standards. In the 16th century the students were birched regularly, and fined a farthing for speaking English and not Latin - but without much success, at least till the 19th century. Academically, the students were most uncooperative, and virtually drowned under the pump any of their colleagues who got anything better than a 'pass' in their degrees; religiously, they were not much better than Richard Barham who never went to chapel in the morning, "Because," he said, "7 a.m. is far too late."

"Too late?" repeated the astonished dean who was questioning him about his absence.

"Oh yes," replied Barham, "I always get to bed by 4 am or 5 am at the latest, and I couldn't possibly stay up till seven - I'd be exhausted the next day!" On the rare occasions when the students did make an effort, they did not get very far. When two of them who had doubts about their religion went to see their tutor at different times, the don was so confused that he told the first to see a doctor because he probably had troubles with his digestion, and the second that he had better join the Church of Rome if he yearned for auricular confession.

Brasenose preferred to devote its time to the appreciation of alcoholic beverages. Every Shrove Tuesday from the year 1700 the butler used to present to the Principal 'ale verses' (in praise of Brasenose ale) written by the best college wits. It was an excess of this ale which provoked a B.N.C. don to challenge a Lincoln don to a duel: the B.N.C. man was killed, and as a result Lincoln college used to allow the Brasenose dons to raid their cellars once a year and drink as much ale as they could in one evening. In 1733 there was another Fellow, Charles Huxley, who was addicted to sack (white wine); in a desperate effort to kick the habit he took to drinking tea... and died a few days later. In the same century there was Sir Tatton Sykes, 'one of the three wonders of Yorkshire, together with York Minster and Fountains Abbey,' who had an unquenchable thirst for ale; he broke stones to increase his appetite and was fond of thrashing impudent bargees.

It was also a B.N.C. man, Alexander Noel (who became Principal and later Dean of St. Paul's) who claimed to have invented 'bottled beer' by leaving it buried in the ground and coming back to find it 'fizzy'. One of the founding members of the Phoenix Wine Club (1781), the oldest social club in Oxford, was Reginald Heber who was more than partial to port. Returning to his room one night, rather tipsy, he collided with a don called Port and fell down; he stated afterwards that it was the only time he was truly 'overcome by port'. He later became Bishop of Calcutta and drowned in his bath in Trichinopoly in 1826. His brother

Richard, also at the college, shared his taste for port and claret but was an even greater lover of books; he died the greatest bibliophile the world has ever seen, leaving a library of 146,827 books stored in six houses throughout the world.

One of the later members of the Phoenix Wine Club, Frodsham Hodson, became Principal of the college in the early 19th century and finally succeeded in making Brasenose the most academic college of its time. He was seen driving into Oxford at the beginning of one term with a coach and four so that it should not be said that 'the first tutor in the first college in the first university in the world entered Oxford with a pair.'

It was at this time, however, that Oxford's most notorious society, The Hell Fire Club, flourished in Brasenose between 1828 and 1834. The dons believed that it was just another wine club; it was in fact a society whose members were dedicated to the worship of the devil, hard drinking and the telling of indecent stories. The truth was dramatically revealed one night when a B.N.C. don, who was returning back from dinner at another college,

PEEPING TOM!

heard screams from a ground floor room, and looking in, saw Edward Trafford (a Hell Fire Club member) struggling with the devil, blue fire, hooves, horns and all. Rushing through the gate, he arrived at the room to be told that Trafford had just collapsed and died of apoplexy.

Brasenose was at one time unquestionably the best rowing college. Its boat was named 'the Child of Hale' after the 9 ft tall Lancashire giant who visited the college in 1617 and left the 17 inch imprint of his hand high up on a cellar wall (Samuel Pepys paid two shillings to see it!). The following rhyme gives the secret of the boat's success:

> *"Queen of the Isis wave,*
> *who trains her crew on beef and beer,*
> *competitors to brave."*

Earl Haig and John Buchan were at Brasenose, and the college has strong American connections. The great-grandfather of the first American president, Lawrence Washington, was here in 1619 and left a buttery bill for 17s 6d which was finally paid by some visiting American lawyers in 1924, and in 1649 the grandfather of the second American president, the Reverend T. Adams, who was deprived of his Fellowship in 1652 for being a Quaker.

To end on a light note, you will be glad to know that the last victim of the Town and Gown riots was Mervyn Prower of Brasenose who was killed in 1851 by a butcher's knife.

NEW COLLEGE

'Manners makyth man' was the motto given to New college in 1379 by its founder William of Wykeham, who intended that the college should provide men for the clergy which had been vastly reduced in numbers by the Black Death. He was a rich churchman himself; it was not manners, however, that made him but his niece, who, people said, was the King's mistress.

OI! MANNERS MAKYTH MAN

BLACK DEATH

The statutes he laid down for New College were worked out to the last detail: it would have no fewer than five deans and three bursars (each keeping an eye on the other) and the largest cesspit in Oxford (which was later carefully 'excavated' and tastefully converted into the students' commonroom); there was to be 'no shooting with arrows, stones, or other missiles, no illicit games, especially games for money, at chess or with ball, no dancing, wrestling and other incautious or inordinate games'; to ensure that his soul, at least, would be saved, the students were to go to church every-day and pray for the founder; and finally, to make absolutely certain that only manners made the New College man, it was even written that the college laundress should be 'of such age and con-dition that no sinister suspicion can, or ought to fall on her'. Oh yes... He generously permitted them (though only on festival days) to sit round a fire and read 'Chronicles of the Realm' and accounts of the 'Wonders of the World'.

The only light relief that the members allowed themselves was to be summoned to meetings by the banging of a wooden mallet at the door of each staircase, and to dinner by two choirboys (of such age and condition etc etc) chanting 'Tempus est vocandi à manger, ô Seigneurs.' (This last practice was thought too frivolous, however, and abandoned in 1830). Life was very grim indeed - a Warden once confined a student to his room for so long that he died of cold and starvation.

Entry to New College was restricted to pupils of Winchester School (also founded by Wykeham) who therefore joined as a matter of course. The epitaph of a Winchester boy, who unfortunately (or fortunately) died in 1676 before he got to New College, ran as follows:

"He was first in the school, and as we hope,
not last in Heaven, whither he went instead of to Oxford."

If the students had a miserable time, the dons certainly did not. The Warden lived in a splendid house and kept six horses; one of them (Warden, not horse) was even in the habit of entertaining for dinner at the High Table ladies of doubtful repute. Erasmus said of the New College Fellow Grocyn that he 'only published one epistle in the whole of his life, for he had so nice a taste that he would rather write nothing than write ill'. This seems to have been the general excuse for the idleness of New College dons. The Warden Dr London, for instance, devoted all his time to astrology which he used in order to track down heretics and personal enemies in other colleges. The dons of the time used to consume vast quantities of negus (hot sweetened wine); when there was a dispute as to whether All Souls or New College served the better negus, a jury of Queen's and Brasenose dons ruled unanimously in favour of New College. "Manners makyth man and the want of them the Fellow"; so the students summed up their seniors.

The most famous Warden of New College was Canon Spooner who invented 'spoonerism' (the art of moving around the first letter of certain words to create a different sense). After a long lecture, he is supposed to have said, "It is tiring work speaking to a row of beery wenches." The longest example attributed to him is his speech to a troublesome undergraduate: "Sir, you have tasted two whole worms; you have hissed all my mystery lectures and you have been caught fighting a liar in the quad. You shall leave by the next town drain." He made his most notorious spoonerism after dinner when he proposed a toast to 'our queer old Dean.' The Warden even extended his spoonerisms to actions: when he was about to board a train at Oxford station, he gave sixpence to the lady who had come to see him off and kissed the porter goodbye.

In the 20th century the students at last achieved some semblance of normality. A don who was particularly disliked was dragged out of his room and crucified on the front lawn with croquet hoops. On another occasion an entrance candidate was confronted at his interview by a small don sitting behind a large newspaper. For a few minutes there was dead silence... then a voice behind the newspaper said;

"Young man, impress me." The candidate hesitated for a moment, then took out his lighter and set fire to the newspaper. He got in . . . but was fined the price of the paper. Another New College man who had done very little work for his examination, handed in a sheet of paper with only his name on it and the following words:

"Fools ask questions which wise men cannot answer."

It is not known whether he passed . . . but even Warden Spooner would have admitted that he was a shining wit.

EXETER COLLEGE

If you ever walk down the Turl towards Trinity at night, you are likely to get a jug of water poured on you from that high building on your right. It may well be your first introduction to Exeter, the college built in 1314 expressly for West country people. It was also one of the first big Whig colleges. During local elections it used to allow Whig voters to pass through its grounds on their way to the polls, and taste its beer. In fact one of the Rectors of Exeter was so keen on Whig principles of democracy that he married the daughter of the college cook.

In the Fellows' Garden at Exeter stands 'Dr. Kennicott's fig tree', so called because Dr. Kennicott, the Greek scholar, hung a "handsoff" label on the one luscious fig which the tree produced that year. Undaunted by the notice, one student was bold enough to pluck the fig and devour it before the good doctor's eyes, saying to his friends, "A fig for Dr. Kennicott."

In the extreme corner of the garden is Bishop Heber's chestnut tree, for which the college pays a yearly rent of £4 to All Souls over whose grounds it spreads its branches. It also used to cast a shade over Bishop Heber's rooms in the neighbouring college of Brasenose (hence the name). On the rare occasions when the tree actually touched Heber's room, it is said, the Exeter boat beat the Brasenose one in the annual race. (This uncommon event occurred in 1895: uncommon, because Brasenose had an excellent rowing team in those days).

So much for Dr. Kennicott's figs and Bishop Heber's nuts...

Lord Shaftesbury was an Exeter man, and is remembered in Oxford for leading a rebellion against the bullying, and 'tucking' of freshmen by older students during his time. ('Tucking' was an initiation rite whereby the victim's lip was scratched, and he was forced to drink a glass of salted water.) He was successful in his efforts, but for the sake of his own safety had to be accompanied by bodyguards from then on. William Morris and Burne-Jones were also Exeter men, and when in 1860 the college pulled down its medieval Chapel and erected a new one at the cost of £9,000, they designed a tapestry for it, entitled "The Adoration of the Magi."

One powermad Exeter dean who read in the ancient college statutes that he could force any college member to attend chapel service, attempted to exercise his authority on one particular don who had never seen the inside of a church and had no wish to; the latter spent half an hour among some large dusty volumes in the library and came up with the solution.

He would be delighted, he said, to attend chapel, on one condition: that the dean also kept to the statutes, and wore at all times a skullcap, a long yellow coat, and yellow stockings... and there the matter rested.

When Farnell the Rector of Exeter retired in 1928, one don asked another whether he knew who the successor would be.

"Well, " replied the other, "I put my money on our friend Dr. Marrett. I notice he has started going to church all of a sudden..." And true enough it was.

A member of Exeter some years ago was the greatnephew of the even greater James Joyce. It is said that at his entrance interview he was asked whether he had read any of his illustrious ancestor's books.

"Oh dear me no!" he is alleged to have replied wittily, "They're far too blasphemous! "

Sometime in the 1970's candidates who had come up to Oxford in the evening for their crucial entrance interview the next day were told by a student pretending to be a scout that if they wanted their shoes cleaned they were to leave them outside their doors before going to bed. At the dead of night, the same student crept round the college, collected all the shoes and threw them into the river...

ORIEL COLLEGE

"When King Edward II of England was fleeing from the battle of Bannockburn he made a vow: If the Blessed Virgin Mary saved his life, he would build a house in Oxford for twenty four students of theology and dedicate it to her; and so it came about that the Hall of the Blessed Mary, or Oriel college, was founded at Oxford."

Magnificent... but unfortunately not quite true. The college was in fact built in 1324 by King Edward's almoner, Adam de Brome, who made him its patron. The King returned the compliment by presenting Oriel with the magnificent gift of a silver drinking cup. His successor, Edward III, kept up this tradition of 'generosity' by presenting the college with St. Bartholomew's leper hospital and the saint's skin which had miraculous powers for curing leprosy.

The name of the college was derived from a ruin on its premises called 'La Oriole'. Indeed, in terms of wealth it was not much better than a ruin. It was poorly endowed - there was not enough silver in the cup, not enough skin on Saint Bartholomew, and not enough lepers in Oxford - and so the college remained poor for a very long time, both financially and intellectually.

Indeed its most eminent member in those antediluvian days, Bishop Butler, threatened to transfer from Oxford to Cambridge because, he wrote, "We are obliged to misspend so much time here in attending frivolous lectures and unintelligible disputations that I am quite tired out with such a disagreeable way of trifling"; but Oriel did try, at least, to make gentlemen of its students.

It succeeded admirably with Sir Walter Raleigh, for example, but another young man was immediately expelled for daring to brush his teeth one morning with elm leaves: this dubious practice was a sure sign, in those days, of homosexuality.

Then we come to the 19th century when Oriel, like quite a few other colleges, flourished. The dons were a powerful intellectual force. Their commonroom, it was said, stank of logic. There was Dr. Pusey, for instance, who had definite High Church learnings. It is alleged that he sacrificed a lamb at the altar every Friday morning. He was not much kinder to women: he described the establishment of the first women's college at Oxford as 'one of the greatest misfortunes that has happened to us even in our own time in Oxford.'

Whately, another Oriel don, was fond of saying that "woman is a creature that cannot reason and pokes the fire from the top." These views may not have been relevant coming from a man who used to walk in Christ Church meadows dressed most unreasonably in a peagreen coat, white waistcoat, stonecoloured shorts and fleshcoloured stockings, at a time when no normal don would be seen dead without his cap and gown. The tobacco hating Provost of Oriel was aghast to find him on the roof one day, quietly smoking cigars among the chimneypots. When he wore holes in his silk stockings he did not bother to get them mended, but stuck black stickingplaster on his legs in the vain hope that people would not notice. He was fond of delivering lectures lying down on a sofa with his legs dangling over the edge, puffing away at a large pipe. In recognition of his qualities Whately was appointed Archbishop of Dublin.

A contemporary of his at Oriel was the famous Cardinal Newman, who used to be the bursar. One year he discovered that there was a mysterious discrepancy in his accounts of between £1,800 and £1,900. Fearing that he would be locked up for embezzling the college funds, he hurriedly took his sheet of figures to the commonroom, to get his colleagues to check it. Nobody could find anything wrong, until the Provost suddenly exclaimed,

"Good heavens, man, don't you see what you've done wrong?"

"No, Provost," replied Newman, baffled.

"Why, on the debit side you've added the date of the year to the pounds, shilling and pence!"

One of Oriel's more famous students was that prince of sartorial elegance, Beau Brummel, who was to die penniless in a Paris attic years later; another was Cecil Rhodes, who was at the time (1873) more concerned with diamond mines than studies, and spent his summer holidays in South Africa. He always looked too wealthy to be a student. Once when a Proctor who wanted to fine him for being out late at night asked him for his name and college, he replied:

"My name is Rhodes and I have just come here from the Cape of Good Hope for a short stay in Oxford; and now, sir, may I ask your name and college?" The Proctor apologised for his mistake and hastily departed.

The most prudish Oriel don was E.E. Genner, even more so than Dr. Pusey. When he was offered port after dinner by Provost Phelps he was horrified.

"I would sooner commit adultery than drink wine!" he declared; and the Provost grinned and replied, "So would we all, Mr. Genner, so would we all."

Finally, Oriel had the somewhat dubious distinction of having the most absentminded (or witty) porters at its gates. A twentieth century tourist who asked for the whereabouts of Cardinal Newman's rooms was told, "I'm sorry, sir, can you please call back later? I don't think he's in at the moment."

CORPUS CHRISTI COLLEGE

he strange-looking obelisk in the front quad of Corpus Christi College is not the spire of yet another underground Church, but a sundial which has witnessed many a strange event. When Dr. Arnold, the famous headmaster of Rugby School, wanted to express his anger, he would throw bottles at this harmless object as it was the only thing that would not fight back.

The founder of Corpus, Bishop Foxe, made the reading of Greek compulsory in his statutes for the students of his college. This 'innovation' lasted for centuries and was cursed by many but carried to an obsession by a few: a Corpus don who wanted to prove that Greek hoplites in the summer of 490 B.C. did in fact run a mile in full armour before fighting the battle of Marathon, had a similar suit of armour made, went to Greece in the height of summer, successfully ran the mile, and then declared that it was a great pity that there was no one there willing to fight him!

Foxe's statutes also specified that every Fellow should share his bedroom with a scholar (the Fellow slept in a comfortable high bed, and the scholar in a truckle bed, and in the morning the scholar made the beds and emptied the chamber pots!). Students had to speak Latin and Greek in hall, and were only allowed to go for walks in groups of three, to play 'games of ball', and carry as weapons bows and arrows. No one but the President was permitted to take his washing to the laundress (and no one but the President ever wanted to). Failure to comply with these rules would result in the student being whipped or placed on a diet of dry bread and water, depending on the gravity of the crime. For attempted murder a scholar was once sentenced to two weeks of dry bread and water (God knows what crime deserved a whipping!)

A prominent Corpus Fellow of the 18th century was Richard Hooker (later Bishop), who was bullied into marrying a battle-axe by the battle-axe's mother. She kept him completely under her thumb - on one occasion some pupils found him reading Horace and tending a flock of sheep in the fields while the shepherd was otherwise employed in the house by the wife.

The 17th century was full of incident. The civil war brought King Charles I to Oxford, and Corpus willingly gave up all its priceless silver plate to be melted down and minted into money for the Royalist cause... or nearly all. Legend has it that the skeleton of the college butler was discovered in a secret cellar clutching the finest piece of all - an enormous silver punch bowl (for whose benefit he was hiding it no one will ever know!). The college was also astonished when in 1653 a large part of the collection was returned anonymously in a hamper. As a result, Corpus today owns the best examples of early silver in Oxford.

Then came the Parliamentary forces and harsh reprisals against Corpus. Many of the Fellows and scholars were expelled. Corpus considered it an ill-omen that the swarm of bees, which had inhabited the college roof for centuries since its foundation, left the same day. One exception was James Quin who sang so well in the presence of Oliver Cromwell that the latter 'liquor'd him with sack', and allowed him to ask for one favour; Quin begged that his scholarship be restored, and this was granted immediately.

During the Restoration a Dr. Newlyn was President of Corpus... and most of the other officials were also Newlyns (he was a disgraceful nepotist). Knowing his relations as he did, he was only moderately perturbed and took no action when one of them crept into a Fellow's bedroom and tried to murder him. He did put his foot down, however, when Matthew Curtois, a Don and a 'Clerk in Holy Orders,' was discovered behaving naughtily with a lady. When Newlyn expelled him, he appealed to King Charles II whose mistress of the time was Nell Gwynne. The King sympathised entirely with Curtois' behaviour, and not only restored him to his Fellowship but also ordered Newlyn to pay him an indemnity.

Corpus men seem to be unusually fond of sermons, good, bad and plain rotten. It was said of President Jackson (1631-40) that he "lived piously, ruled peaceably, wrote profoundly and preached painfully." In the 18th century, a Corpus Fellow preached a long sermon in which he denounced 'red' as the colour of Satan; it was unfortunately delivered on a Scarlet Day when the Vice-Chancellor and his Doctors had to sit uncomfortably through it in their bright red robes. Dr. Fowler, President in the 19th century, once fined a Fellow eight sermons for looking lustfully at a beauty.

The college was ashamed to have had the Duke of Monmouth as a student in 1665, and later struck his name off the register when he led his infamous rebellion against the Crown. Among its better loved sons were General Oglethorpe (the founder of the American state of Georgia), Keble (of college fame), and Ruskin who declared, when he was moving from Christ Church (Aedes Christi, the House of Christ) to Corpus Christi, that he was merely moving from the House of Christ to the Body of Christ. What a wit!

WORCESTER COLLEGE

Because of its distance from other colleges, Worcester has been unfairly called 'the Botany Bay' of Oxford. This arises from the fact that before Beaumont Street was built there was only one way to get to it, through Friar's Entry, a narrow passage teeming with scruffy urchins, mad dogs and angry washerwomen dodging the contents of the evil-smelling pots emptied from the windows above, and across Gloucester Green which was then - vive la difference! - a pig market.

In more recent times wicked people have maintained that Worcester's only contribution to the 'city of learning' is the clock on its facade, indispensable to the traveller hurrying on his way to the railway station; adding insult to injury, a Keble undergraduate once addressed a letter to 'Worcester College, near Oxford.' Enough of this slander. Although very poor - it has only a twentieth of the wealth of Christ Church - Worcester has a beautiful front quad, delightful gardens and a very pretty lake with ducks and geese. Watch out for the geese: they do not like bare legs and have been known to chase visitors in shorts round and round the very pretty lake...

But now for some vital statistics:

Founded in the 13th century as Gloucester Hall, it was a monastic establishment till 1541 for monks who wanted to lead a strict and pious life of prayer and study... and very pious it was too. In 1539 four monks were arrested for attempting to murder the Proctor, while another was discovered to have consumed, with the aid of a bookseller, twenty legs of mutton, five rounds of beef and six capons, all this between Ash Wednesday and Good Friday. After the dissolution of monasteries, Gloucester Hall began to accept laymen. One of these was Thomas Coryate, the man who brought table forks, fans and umbrellas to England and who finally died in 1617 from drinking too much 'sack'.

The 17th Century saw Gloucester Hall's darkest years; the Arts flourished - Black Arts. The unquestioned master of these satanic rites was Thomas Allen, mathematician and necromancer extraordinaire (skilled in the art of prediction by communicating with the dead), who was so skilful that his scout, poor man, saw 'spirits coming upstairs like bees to assist him in his sorcery'. His most promising pupil was Sir Kenelm Digby who prepared a devilish ointment guaranteed to take off

VANISHING CREAM!

years from one's age when applied to the face. He tried it on his wife: it took off ears, nose and virtually everything else... and to cut a long story short, she died.

Richard Lovelace, however, who was here in 1634, needed no ointment to improve his looks - it was said of him that 'he was the most amiable and beautiful person that eye ever beheld'. So pretty in fact that the Queen was persuaded by one of her ladies-in-waiting to confer upon him a Master of Arts degree because 'he had greatly enhanced the beauty of Oxford'. He is the author of the immortal line 'stone walls do not a prison make', which he wrote when imprisoned as a Royalist in 1640. In 1690, a certain Worcestershire man, Sir Thomas Cookes, left £10,000 for the establishment of either a workhouse or a college in Oxford, this money was acquired by the authorities of Gloucester Hall who succeeded admirably in combining the two... and so Worcester College was born.

One of its first and worst pupils was Samuel Foote, the comedian, who in 1737 wangled a scholarship as 'founder's kin', claiming that his great-grandfather was the founder's second cousin. His stay was short but colourful; Foote never toed the line with the Provost, Dr. Gower, whom he once pursued mimicking down the High Street dressed as Punch, to the delight of Dr. Johnson who was present. On another occasion he tied hay to a bell-rope hanging in a church porch which opened on a field where cattle grazed. When the bell started ringing furiously at the dead of night, the Provost and his Bulldog rushed to the scene, fearing supernatural influences, to find a cow tugging impatiently at the rope in her attempts to eat the hay. The Provost realised immediately who was to blame, but on being accused Foote flatly denied responsibility. But the Provost was to have the last word: Foote was seen driving a 'coach and six' at great speed down the High Street with a scantily clad actress on his lap, and, what shocked the Provost most, without wearing his cap and gown. Foote finally admitted defeat and was sent down.

DISGRACEFUL!
NO CAP
OR GOWN!

In 1803 Thomas de Quincey, the poet, arrived at Worcester with only fifty guineas in his pocket to last him his entire stay in Oxford. He claimed that he only uttered a hundred words in his first two years in college; this was perhaps the result of his famous toothache for which a friend recommended opium as a painkiller. The advice proved fatal. He became incurably addicted to opium and even though he wrote a brilliant final paper, it caused him to lose confidence and flee from Oxford before his oral examination.

The early 20th century found Worcester in a dangerously sporty mood. A favourite game of the time was to release a cage-full of rats in the front quad and attack them with hockey sticks. It was wise to show some interest in this and other Worcester activities: one undergraduate, who refused to run along the tow-path and support the college boat, was dragged out of his room in his evening clothes (after his locked door had been battered down) and thrown howling into the very pretty lake where he was followed by the greater part of his belongings. However, a final word of warning to those of you who are excessively sporty: remember the Worcester man 'sconced' in 1948 for saying that the Hall looked like the interior of a Wedgewood teapot; he chose whisky as his drink and, after emptying two pints of it without pause for breath, fell down dead.

KEBLE COLLEGE

eble College has to be seen to be believed. Built of red brick with cream-coloured patterns, it is sometimes called 'zebra college', and its architecture has been described as 'early bloody'. Tennyson thought the college looked 'most indecent' and Ruskin used to make detours to avoid it on his daily walk.

Unusual among colleges because it has horizontal corridors instead of the usual vertical staircases, Keble was built to combine plain living with High Church (almost Roman Catholic) thinking. The Keble wit who wrote a letter to 'Worcester College, near Oxford' received a stinging reply addressed to 'Keble College, near Rome'.

A Keble undergraduate obviously unused to plain living, demanded a quart of beer in the middle of an exam because he had found out
that the University statutes entitled him to it; he received his beer after
much clamouring, but was promptly fined by the Proctor for not wearing a sword in the examination hall (also a statutory requirement).

There is a place near Oxford on the river Cherwell called 'Parson's
Pleasure' where dons used to bathe naked; women were expressly forbidden entry. One fine afternoon, however, a punt laden with giggling
undergraduates (female and male) floated past, to the great embarrass-
ment of the bathers who hurriedly wrapped towels around their waists;
but one Keble don merely covered his face and on being asked why,
replied, "Oh, *my* pupils know me by my *face.*"

Some years ago, Gerard McHugh, a young man desiring to join
Keble, attended his entrance interview one morning, after a night of
drunken revelry (and maccaroni-cheese), feeling distinctly ill. After a
few minutes of pleasant conversation, he was asked,

"And now Mr. McHugh, what do you think of this college?" Unable to control himself any longer, McHugh was violently sick all over the floor... Needless to say he was not accepted by the college.

ST. EDMUND HALL

ne of the oldest foundations in Oxford St. Edmund Hall (1269) better known as Teddy Hall only became a college in 1957. It is worth a mention because one man of absolutely phenomenal importance went there: Paul Methuen who in 1703 signed a Treaty with Portugal and so introduced port and gout into Oxford... which means England.

HERTFORD COLLEGE

ertford has the most complex and chaotic history of any Oxford college. It started life in the 13th century as Hart Hall, a sort of glorified boarding-house for self-styled students. One of these was called the 'Principal', and his sole duty was to collect rents from his colleagues which he then handed over to the landlord at the end of the month. This happy state of affairs continued well into the 18th century, with remarkably few events of any note. The poet John Donne was here in 1584 and having done whatever it was he wanted to do, he left. Then there was that enterprising young woman in 1617 who gained entry by dressing up as a man, but the authorities soon got wise to her supernumerary charms, and she was banished.

With the arrival in 1737 of the dynamic Dr. Newton (no, not Isaac, Richard) Hart Hall was transformed into a proper college (Hertford College) and began to attract important people. There was James Foxe, the politician, who once jumped out of a college window to join a town-and-gown fight. He was so short of money during one summer holiday that he walked from Oxford to London and sold his gold watch to pay for lunch on the way. When a friend remarked to him that it was pleasant to lie in the grass with a book, he gave the famous reply that it was even more pleasant to lie in the grass without a book. There was also George Selwyn who was expelled from university for parodying the rites of Holy Communion during a wine club meeting.

The success of Hertford College was short-lived, however. It had poor endowments - its Fellows were only paid fifteen pounds a year and its Head sixty - and nobody came to replace the old dons when they died. Eventually there was one batty old gentleman left, by the name of Hewitt (a self-elected Vice-Principal), who when they came to take him away, protested loudly that he wanted to be left alone to die in peace; and this he finally did...

It was then that a crafty solicitor called Robertson moved into the vacant premises as (yet another) self-styled caretaker. More squatters followed, each the caretaker of his own little room, until part of the building collapsed under the weight of caretakers. At this point the university stepped in, evicted the squatters (what was left of them) and turned over the property to Magdalen Hall. This was an establishment with an even more dubious reputation than Hart Hall. Its students could stay for as long as they liked, as long as they paid their rent. There is a limerick which runs:

> *A member of Magdalen Hall,*
> *Who knew next to nothing at all;*
> *He was fifty-three*
> *When he took his degree*
> *Which was youngish for Magdalen Hall.*

It did, however, have its share of distinguished people: in the 17th century, there was Thomas Hobbes, the political philosopher, who 'vastly preferred catching birds (whatever that might mean) to studying philosophy'

in his youth. At the age of ninety-one he used to sing 'prick songs' in bed (whatever that might mean) 'to keep his lungs healthy', which exasperated the Dean of Christ Church who told him "that he was an old man with one foot in the grave, that he should mind his latter end (whatever that might mean) and not trouble the world any more with his papers."

TIME FOR A 'PRICK SONG'
METHINKS

Jonathan Swift, the author of 'Gulliver's Travels', was Dean of Magdalen Hall in 1692. A lawyer asked him one day who would win if there was a fight between the clergy and the Devil. "The Devil," he thundered, "because all the lawyers are on his side." In a more light-hearted moment he is supposed to have stated that "Wisdom is a hen whose cackling we must value and consider because it is attended with an egg."

In 1816 Magdalen Hall was burned down after a riotous students' party (someone passed his degree at the age of forty five) and all its members moved to the buildings of the now extinct Hertford College. It was at this time that it accepted its most eccentric character, Robert Hawker, the poet of Morwenstow. When his father warned him that he could no longer afford to keep him in college, he leapt on to his horse and rode to Bude where his beautiful godmother lived... well, she may not have been beautiful but at least she had an income of £200 a year. He asked for her hand in marriage, and she graciously accepted (the fact that she was twenty-one years older did not seem to worry him). Nevertheless, the marriage was a happy one: and if he wore a pink hat without a brim at her funeral, it was not out of disrespect, but eccentricity.

In the 19th century halls went out of fashion: Magdalen Hall became a college in 1874 . . . yes, again Hertford College! Surprisingly, it is still Hertford College today. Evelyn Waugh was here in the 1920's. He hated his tutor, C. Cruttwell, and this is perhaps why a curious character called Cruttwell appears as a villain in most of his early novels.

The misfortunes that have befallen the Hertford buildings through the ages were not over even recently: there was the saga of the spin-dryer. The college once spent £1000 on a new laundry room and equipment; but they forgot one little detail... the doors were not made wide enough to allow the spin-dryer through, and so it remained outside, probably still to this day, rusting away.

THE WOMEN'S COLLEGES

I n the beginning there was man, in Oxford; only man. Then in 1877, God, or it may have been the Vice-Chancellor, decreed that dons (who had remained celibate till then) would henceforth be allowed to marry. It was the beginning of the End . . .

In 1878, the first of the female dons and under-graduates appeared in Oxford and colleges had to be built to house them: notoriously blue-stocking Somer-ville, for instance, with its forbidding Porteress and even more forbidding walls within which an unsus-pecting policeman was once trapped after mid-night by crafty members of the col-lege. This academi-cally first-rate institu-tion, one of whose members was Margaret Thatcher, the ex-Prime Minister of Great Britain, chose for its emblem six daggers and three red stars: daggers which broke your heart and stars which you saw, when the women jilted you.

Almost as intellectual was Lady Margaret Hall, but not quite. One of its members who for some reason wanted to fail her finals, sat for only one of a total of nine papers: to her disgust she actually passed, because (she was told) one had to get nine C's to fail and she only got one.

Then there was the women's college by the river, St. Hilda's, whose members (it is alleged) went to sleep on the last day of April every year with strings tied to their toes and dangling out of the windows over the river: they were woken the next morning by their men-friends who twitched the threads as they punted past the college down the river to Magdalen, to listen to the May morning carol service that was sung from Magdalen Tower.

Women may have been tolerated in those days but their behaviour was certainly restricted. They could only ride bicycles in pairs; and if they wanted to play tennis they went to the courts in bath-chairs as it was 'unseemly' for them to be seen walking down the streets with tennis-racquets.

Women were finally allowed to take degrees in 1920 (27 years, it must be added, before their Cambridge counterparts) but their ultimate triumph was only achieved as late as 1963 when that last bastion of male supremacy, the Oxford Union Debating Society, gave way and admitted them as members.

WADHAM COLLEGE

Nicholas Wadham, a childless landowner from Somerset, was coaxed in 1610 into founding this college by an enthusiastic neighbour. After making all plans, however, he disappointed everyone by dying, and it was left to his wife Dorothy (who unfortunately was also childless) to carry out his wishes; a great stroke of luck, indeed, for Wadham, because Dorothy seems to have been a truly emancipated woman, as shown by her college statutes which were unbelievably liberal for the time. Since then Wadham has always maintained this free-and-easy tradition: it was one of the first colleges for instance, to intro-duce women into its curriculum.

When the poet Matthew Arnold was at Oxford, and even years later at the age of sixty, he was very fond of jumping over one particular fence in Wadham because, he said, the college had that sort of effect on him. Of its own famous people Wadham has had many. Thomas Sydenham the so-called founder of medicine, Admiral Blake who was embarrassingly Parliamentarian at a time when the college was staunchly Royalist, Cecil Day Lewis and Sir Thomas Beecham; also Joseph Trapp, the first Professor of Poetry who wrote in 1715 the well-known verse which

Oxford occasionally likes to sling at its counterpart Cambridge:

The King, observing with judicious eyes,
The State of both his Universities,
To Oxford sent a troop of horse; and why?
That learned body wanted loyalty.
To Cambridge books he sent as well discerning
How much that loyal body wanted learning.

Also a member of Wadham was The Wicked Earl of Rochester who wrote on Charles II's door when he was in Oxford:

Here lies a great and mighty King,
Whose promise none relied on.
He never said a foolish thing,
Nor ever did a wise one.

Charles II, quite unperturbed, replied with the comment that his words were his own while his deeds were those of his ministers.

The most distinguished pupil of all, however, was Sir Christopher Wren the renowned architect who was also Wadham's Professor of Astronomy. Apart from such Oxford architectural triumphs as Tom Tower in Christ Church and the Sheldonian Theatre (which he designed as a Roman Theatre with a hanging roof), he made the first model of the moon and invented a method of blood transfusion for animals.

Not quite a famous man but definitely an infamous one was Warden Symmons, head of Wadham from 1831 to 1871. A very holy man he used to maintain that a lack of belief was no justification for not taking Holy Orders. At Chapel service every day he would fill his pockets with money received in the collection. He said, and no one doubted him, that it would go to a needy cause. His wife used to hold extraordinarily 'chummy' prayer-meetings in her drawing-room, and kept a pet cow, whose milk was supplied at exorbitant cost to the undergraduates; the proceeds were to go to the 'propagation of the Gospel in foreign parts'. (Perhaps she considered her husband a foreign part).

MORE 'FOREIGN PARTS' MONEY

One of the good Warden's pupils was Barnett, the founder of the 'Socialist Movement', who caused an uproar by earnestly suggesting at an Oxford Union Debate that the only way to civilise the East End of London was for Oxford men to colonise it.

In 1880, the success of the college boat on the river was celebrated by the students with an enormous bonfire on the prize college lawn. The authorities were furious and promptly cancelled the annual college concert as a punishment. The students retaliated by breaking into the rooms (at the dead of night) of 'Unbelieving Dick' an unpopular college don who was pursued in his night-shirt across the aforementioned (charred) front lawn by hoards of blood-thirsty brats. To track down the villains responsible for this outrage the college employed a private detective who was unfortunately detected himself and pitilessly punished under the college pump. The authorities then played their trump card by sending down the whole college.

On the 21st of November 1928 some Wadham jokers sent messages to over 1000 students saying that the Proctor wanted to see them at 9.45 a.m. outside the Sheldonian Theatre. When the students had duly assembled, the Wadham men phoned up the police and the Proctors to say that there was a riot at the Sheldonian and would they please do something, and the Fire Station to say that there was a fire and would they please do something, and then sat back to enjoy the resulting chaos, with thousands of perplexed and irate people arguing and shouting amidst whistles, sirens and roaring fire engines.

On a more recent occasion Wadham students bought vast quantities of spoilt fish from the Oxford market which were allowed to decay even further in the sun, and then 'posted' them in every pillar-box in the town. Her Majesty's Post Office thought that it was a rotten joke.

The last comment about the college comes from a friend of R. Dawkins, the professor who fell dead outside Wadham. When told of his death the friend remarked, "Sad, isn't it?... And even sadder to think that he chose to die outside *Wadham!*"

JESUS COLLEGE

Even though the college was founded in 1571 for the natives of Wales by Hugh Price, a Welshman who started life as a butcher, it is not true that Jesus College is still a 'little Wales' in Oxford. Nor is it true that they cultivate leeks on one side of the front lawn and feed goats on the other. It is also quite untrue that if you stand next to the goats among the leeks and shout 'Jones' at the top of your voice, a hundred different enquiring faces will suddenly appear out of windows and door-ways . . . (try instead, David or Llewellyn).

But leeks are nevertheless prominent vegetables in the college's history. A leek is still hoisted on the college flag-pole every St. David's day (the patron saint of Wales, of course), and on that day, up to the last century, a green leek was attached to the tassel of the cap of every student by his servant. Most of the students would then attend their Chapel service and lectures with their leeks flapping about, but the more daring and patriotic actually ventured down the High Street where more often than not their vegetables suffered unspeakable fates at the hands of vandals.

Another college tradition is connected with the enormous silver punch bowl which was presented to Jesus in 1732 by a former student, Sir William Wynne: it is 5 ft in circumference and holds ten gallons. There is a tradition that anyone, whose arms are long enough to be able to encircle the punch bowl and who has the capacity to drink its contents in one go, can then walk away with the bowl as his own, although some-one once succeeded in encircling it with his arms, no one has managed the ten gallons yet... This pastime must have helped in getting the members of Jesus described as 'Welshmen who were more physical than spiritual'. For many centuries, the college was little known and lived in a world of its own because its benefactions were restricted to Welshmen, who tended to stay away from the rest of the university. There is the story of the don from Jesus who made an order at a shop and asked for it to be delivered to the college. The salesgirl wrote down his name, paused and then asked:

"Excuse me, sir, but how do you spell 'Jesus'?" Then there is the American tourist who found that Jesus College had no outstanding char-acteristic or features and told the porter that 'he could never tell the dif-ference between Lincoln and Jesus', whereupon the porter sourly answered him: "Sir, no American can."

The notorious Beau Nash, 'King' of Bath, was an undergraduate here for a very short time; there are two versions as to why he was sent down. The first states that he was deeply involved in a love affair (which almost ended up in marriage) with a wily woman before he was seven-teen; the second that he ran away from college with his 'quarter's allowance' and earned his living by doing 'something ridiculous' for a wager. His favourite act was to ride through a village on a cow, stark naked. Just as well he never tried it in Oxford!

Nothing is ever taken seriously at Oxford, not even death. One Jesus Principal, Dr. Joseph Hoare, died in 1802 as a result of a tragic accident: he unintentionally put his chair on the tail of the college cat which screeched in pain and bit his leg. The bite proved to be fatal. Dr. Hoare was said to have been 'cat-martyred' and the inevitable poetical epitaph was composed by the students:

> *"Poor Dr. Hoare is no more*
> *Bid the harpstrings of Cambria mourn;*
> *the Head of a house died the death of a mouse,*
> *And Tom must be hanged in return."*

Henry Vaughan, the poet, was at Jesus in the 17th century, and was accused of being a 'poor-spirited' person for refusing to fight for the king in the Civil War because he preferred 'poetry to pistols.' Another poet, who came much later in the 19th century, was Sir Lewis Morris. Poor Sir Lewis, whose mediocre poetry was not in great demand, once told Oscar Wilde that he thought he was the victim of a 'conspiracy of silence', and asked Oscar what he would advise him to do. Oscar Wilde with his usual tact answered:

"My dear fellow, I would advise you to join this conspiracy."

T.E. Lawrence (that man of Arabia) was also an undergraduate here. He must have had something against All Souls as he is said to have drawn lengthy plans to plant mushrooms and to keep a herd of stolen deer (surely from Magdalen) in their quadrangle.

It was at this time that the neighbouring Exeter college was made to show its respect for the 'Welsh College'. Some Jesus students had gone into Exeter hall and covered all the benches with a thick coat of marmalade. The Exeter students, coming in to dinner, said grace standing up as usual, and then sat down... only to jump up immediately in great discomfort to be confronted with a notice nailed to the reverse of the door, which said:

"STAND UP FOR JESUS."

Harold Wilson, a Socialist ex-Prime Minister of Great Britain, was a student of the college many, many years ago when he was also a member of the Liberal Club... and the fact that he was tolerated for so long is a great credit to the college. But then, Jesus men (and women) have always been tolerant.

There is the story of the student (drunk, of course) who was trying in the middle of the night to get back to his own room across the college roof-top. In his drunken stupor he made a mistake and lowered himself through the window into the Principal's bedroom. The Principal's wife woke up, startled, and was about to cry out when the student put a finger in front of his mouth and whispered: "Sssh! You'll wake up the Principal," and departed as quickly as he came...

And may we depart with him, leaving you with the words of Her Majesty Queen Victoria:

"Oxford... that old monkish place which I have a horror of."